BEST FISHING LURES FOR FRESHWATER FISH

How to catch more Bass, Pike, Muskie, Panfish Walleye and Trout

ABOUT THIS BOOK

This book is set up like my other books. This is a reference guide you can use to see what the best lures are to use for the fish you are going after. I will show you the lures to use to have the greatest chance to catch fish when you hit the water.

Do you want to know the most likely lures to use when you go fishing? These tips will give you the best chances to catch fish when you are on the lake. All of us that are not professional fishermen all have the same goal. We want to catch as many fish as we can, when we get the time to fish.

You can read through the whole book at one time, and I recommend that you do. I wrote this book so you can use it as a quick reference for the fish you will fish for, and the best lures to use for those fish. Furthermore, you should have at least one of each of the go to lures for all the fish in the summary at the end of the book you fish for. You should always have them with you. So, if what you are using is not working, you can tie one of them on and catch fish when no one else is getting any fish.

My goal when I go fishing is the same as most of you have for a goal. I want to catch the most fish in the limited time I spend on the water. This book will help you do that, and you can find the information fast to help you catch fish.

TABLE OF CONTENTS

BASS
PIKE
MUSKIE
PANFISH
WALLEYE
TROUT
SUMMARY

BASS LURES

SPINNERBAITS

Spinner baits are by far the most-used baits for bass. Fishermen love them, and bass love them too. This is not itself a spinner bait. However, it is an important part of the spinner bait. These are the best skirts I have ever used. I use them for spinnerbait skirts and jig skirts. **They are Terminator power pulse skirts.** Check them out, they are awesome.

Johnson Beetle Spin

This is one of my all-time favorite lures to catch all kinds of fish. If I had to pick one lure and one lure only for fishing, I would pick the beetle spin. It is one of the most versatile baits you can have. For bass, I like purple, black and white. I use it with the split tail or curly tail bodies. It comes through weeds well and will get bit and hooked better than safety pin type spinner baits. You can take off the spinner blade and use it as a jig. There are saltwater versions I use for bass and pike. If you want bigger baits, get the salt version.

I have caught hundreds of bass and pike, and many walleye, panfish, and even a carp on this lure. **Here is a video of a kid**

catching a 6 plus pound bass on a beetle spin.

Booyah Pikee Spinnerbait

This is one of my favorite spinnerbaits for pike. This bait catches a lot of fish. It is also one of the few spinner baits that has the twisted wire attachment point. This lets you connect to the spinner bait with your line or leader, and it does not move up the wire and get tangled on the cast.

I know they say it is stronger not to twist the wire. They say it is cheaper for the manufacturers to make them without the twist. I like the twist and not having to put something around the wire to keep the line in place. It also comes in great colors and the thinner head makes it rip through weeds easier and with less hang-ups.

This lure is also a great bass spinnerbait, and the double willow leaf blades add the right amount of flash. This is a ½ oz bait.

Strike King mini king

The strike king mini king is another of my favorite bass spinnerbaits. If you need a smaller bait, this is the one. If you put a curly tail grub on it, you can add enough bulk to make it an amazingly effective mid-size bait that will attract bass.

Northland Reed Runner

This is my most used spinnerbait of this type. It works great for bass and pike, and you can fish it anywhere. I like the ¼ oz or ⅜ oz. white shad, and I put a 3 or 4 in Twister tail grub on it. The Canary color with a yellow twister tail grub is great for pike. Northland lure company is in Bemidji Minnesota.

Northland Mimic Minnow Spin

This is another great spinnerbait; it is the same style as the beetle spin. This one has more of a real minnow look, and it comes in more sizes. This bait is also usable in many situations. You can fish it without the spinner, and it is a great swimbait. It will also catch a variety of fish. Because of the shape of the body and the head, it is not as weedless as the beetle spin.

CRANKBAITS

Crankbaits catch a lot of bass. Crankbaits cover many types of lure that cover a variety of situations of fishing. You can fish them from shallow to deep and everywhere between. Most crankbaits give a depth the bait will dive to. That depth is most of the time a max depth. Plan on the bait not going as deep as max depth.

Mann's 1 minus

This is a cool crankbait you can use in places most others cannot be used. This crankbait is usable over weed tops and when the fish are in shallow water. The bait is a good size for a shallow diver. It has bulk to attract bigger fish but stays shallow. You can crank it slow, crank it fast, or twitch it back and forth and use it as a topwater lure. It is versatile and catches fish.

Norman's deep little N

This is a great crankbait. I have been using this bait for 30 years. I have a baby bass color one I have had and used for over 20 years. It has several teeth marks from pike biting it. This is a deep diving crankbait, but I often use it in a way that is kind of unconventional.

There is a lake I fish often. The south end of the lake is all sandy bottom. I have found that using this bait in 2 to 4 feet of water and letting it bounce along the bottom has caught me a lot of fish. I use it near the edges of reed beds that grow in the sandy bottom. The bass come out of the reeds to go after the bait. Even a few pike lurk in these reeds. Try it if you know an area like this.

The bait is also great around deep structure or trolling in 10 to 12 feet of water along weed lines.

Storm Wiggle Wart

This bait is my favorite mid-size crankbait for warmer water. It contains rattles that attract fish, and it has a wider wobble that works better in warmer water. I love this bait for fishing 4 to 8 feet deep. It will catch as most crankbaits a variety of fish, lots of bass and pike.

Strike King Square Bills

Square billed crankbaits should be part of your arsenal for catching bass. They will stay shallow, move back and forth, and bounce off obstructions on the bottom. This bait works great in moving water areas. Rivers always have snags on the bottom. This style of bait will bounce off most of them. This bait also works great in shallow areas with a rocky bottom, and over the top of weeds. There are several manufactures who make square bills, I like the strike king brand best. They come in a couple of different sizes and more colors than you could ever use. My favorites are the perch and the chili craw.

Rapala Shadow Rap

This is a unique lure. It is a jerk bait crankbait that imitates an injured fish. If you stop the retrieve the bait will rise. Then a little twitch and the bait will turn and dart side to side like an injured fish. You also can keep the lure in the strike zone much longer. You can work it without moving it extremely far. It will stay in the strike zone longer on the way back to the boat.

Lipless Crankbaits

The Rat-l-trap is the most well-known and is a great lure. There are several other companies that make effective lipless crankbaits. Rapala makes the rattling and ripping raps that work well at catching bass and pike. These baits have a tight wobble that is better in colder water than a wide wobbling bait. They also work well in warmer water. This bait can also work at almost any depth, let it sink to the depth you want and fish. If you crank it right away when it hits the water, you can keep it shallow.

Rapala Shad Rap

Many fishermen have said this is the best fishing lure ever made. I do not know if I would go that far, but it is one of the best lures for many types of fish. This is one of the best bass crankbaits there is. The way the lure moves also makes walleyes want to eat it.

This lure comes in a multitude of colors. It comes in six different sizes from 1 ½" up to 3 ½ inches, and dives from 5 to 15 feet.

The black and silver and the perch are my favorite colors. This lure is a great casting and trolling lure and runs true out of the box. This is one of my go to lures for bass because when I use it, I often catch pike, bass and walleyes in the same areas. **Here is a video that shows you how to fish it.**

TOPWATER

Fishing topwater lures for bass is the most exciting type of bass fishing. It gets the adrenaline flowing when a bass comes out of the water to smash your bait. Most of these topwater lures have been around for a long time. They have been because they catch fish. Topwater lures in dark colors work best. The dark silhouette against the light sky makes a better visual for the bass.

Live Target weedless frog

I have used the snag proof original weedless frog and have caught fish on it. However, my favorite now is the live target hollow body frog. The bait looks so real and comes in a variety of colors. The thing that sets this bait above the others is the realistic look and vivid colors. Along with the lifelike rubber strands that look like frog legs moving around in the water. A great bass attracter.

Zara Spook

This topwater bait has been around since the 1940s. It is still a popular topwater lure and catches a lot of bass. You can work it over weeds and structure having it swing right to left. It stays over the strike zone area longer, giving the fish more opportunities to hit it. The action is great for bass and pike. You can get it with the original look. They also make a spook with dual props.

Hula Popper

This lure made by Arbogast, made by a fisherman who wanted a topwater lure he could use. Fred Arbogast made the hula popper and the Jitterbug. The originals carved by him by hand. He started the company in 1928.

This is one of my favorite topwater lures. The popping creates a sound that bass cannot resist. The frog like look gives it a great visual attraction as well. It looks as best topwater lures look, like a dying fish or a frog that is struggling on the surface to survive. It is easy to fish and fun because the strikes are so vicious and unexpected. You need to stay alert fishing this bait.

Smithwick Devil's Horse

There are several propeller topwater baits, but the devil's horse is the best. It is like a buzz bait; however, you can vary the way you fish it. You can fish it fast or slow, both ways work well at different times. There is another prop bait I use that I like a lot, the **Heddon Tiny torpedo**. This bait is smaller and more like a short spook with a single prop in back.

Rebel pop-r

This is another great topwater lure. You can use it, so it keeps the lure over the area where the fish are for a longer time. Cast and let it sit for a few seconds. Give it a twitch and it will pop creating a splash and sound, then let it sit again. Keep doing this while it is over the spot you think the fish are. Get ready, the hits can be explosive.

Jitterbug

This lure also hand made at the beginning by Fred Arbogast, he created it for himself to catch fish. It has stood the test of time for almost 90 years, and it still catches fish. It is one of the easiest lures to fish. You cast it and reel it back. The lure does the work of wobbling side to side and making a sound that bass have a hard time resisting. Check out the link in the Jitterbug heading to see a great deal on Amazon for a three pack of very usable topwater lures.

Booyah Buzz bait

Buzz baits work to catch bass in the right conditions. This bait is one of the best. It has good action and a clacker that makes even more noise to attract the fish. You can get buzz baits with single or double spinners. As far as buzz baits go, I prefer in line baits. There are a few brands available. **My favorite is a Floyds buzzer**. They are getting hard to find. I have had one for many years and I like it. I have found another one I like that is similar. **The buzz saw.**

JIGS

Jigs have always been great baits for bass. Jigs are the best bait there is if you are looking to catch your biggest bass. More big bass get caught on jigs than any other bait. There are hundreds of brands available, many of them look similar. The things that make one jig better than another, are better skirts. Better colors, better heads and better weed guards.

Nu Tech Jigs

I saw these jigs, and I thought they looked cool, so I thought I would try them. I have a great story about them. It was the middle of May 2015. I had gotten and new Shimano worm and jig rod and a new Shimano spinning reel. I prefer to fish jigs and worms with spinning gear. I went to the lake, walked down to the shore where the dock goes, I put the jig on the line. 3/8 oz watermelon red skirt. My first cast with my new rod and reel and a new jig and I caught this beast of a bass. A 5 lb. 4 oz bass in Minnesota is a great bass. Hard to top that. It was my birthday as well.

You can also get the Nu Tech naked head ones and put the **Terminator power pulse skirts on them for a great jig.**

Terminator Jigs

This is the only bass jig I use other than the Nu tech. The terminator jigs use the same fantastic jig skirts I use for the spinnerbaits. The heads are nice also because they do not hang up on anything and they stand up great on the bottom.

WORMS

Tom Mann said, "I will fish any color worm, as long as it's black". Black is a good color choice if nothing else is working. I do not think it is the best color in all situations.

Worms are huge in the world of bass fishing. If you want to have the best chances of catching the most bass. And if you want to be the best bass fisherman you can be, you need to be a worm fisherman. There are hundreds of types of worms and thousands of colors. All of them will catch fish. Some of them will catch lots of fish much of the time.

Worms have won more bass tournaments than any other lures. Most pro fishermen are top worm fishermen. They know they must catch bass with worms to win tournaments. These are the ones, I and several top worm fishermen feel are the best worms to do that.

Mann's Jelly Worms

This is the worm that changed bass fishing forever. Before Tom Mann created the jelly worms. Bass worms were hard and lifeless, they were more like tire rubber. They caught bass, but they were difficult to use, and they did not smell good. They smelled like rubber.

Mann made them soft and lifelike and they smelled good. And they caught a lot of bass. The electric grape has always been my favorites for clear water. The hard nose version is worth a try also, they may be better than the originals.

Gambler Sweebo Worms

The June bug and green pumpkin are my favorite choice. They are also the most popular color choice of these worms. Watermelon red is the next most popular choice. This worm is highly effective in clear and muddy water and will work with any worm rigging. Prices for these worms differ from seller to seller. Make sure you check prices to get the best deal. Tackle warehouse has the best prices on them most of the time.

Robo Worms

The strait tail robo worm is my favorite finesse worm. You can fish it weightless Texas rigged and pull it through the tops of the weeds and catch a ton of bass. It is also a great drop shot worm. Great after a cold front when the bass shut down.

Yum Lures F2 Dinger Bait

This is my favorite stick worm. These work great fished wacky or Texas rigged. I like to use them weightless; they are heavier and have a slow sink. Because they are bigger around, the give a look of a bigger bait. They are more expensive than Senko worms, but they are tougher and will last much longer. The Yum worms are salt infused, and that is also an added attractant to catch more fish.

Creme Scoundrel Worm

Nick Creme made the first plastic worms. He made them from a mold he made from a real nightcrawler. The Creme scoundrel is a kind of cross between the Mann's Jelly worm and the Gambler Sweebo. This is another worm I have used with success.

OTHER SOFT PLASTICS

There are many other types of soft plastic baits that will catch fish. Some of them are great. Some are more of a novelty. These are the ones worth checking out. They will catch you fish, sometimes better than any other bait.

Swimbaits are favorites of many fishermen now and growing in popularity all the time. Swimbaits come in three forms, hard body, soft body, and paddle tail baits. The soft body swimbaits are the best. There are so many crankbaits that hard body swimbaits are like crankbaits with a soft body. I am not saying they are not good. I have a multi jointed hard swimbait I use occasionally and have caught a few fish on it, but it is not one of my top choices.

Storm's Wildeye swimbaits

This is a great versatile bait that will catch most types of fish. It comes in several sizes and color combinations. This is my favorite swimbait. I cast the lure and let it settle to the bottom. Then give it a flick and crank it, stop, and start every few handles turns to make it look injured. I also sometimes put a large saltwater beetle spin spinner on it and fish it like a big meaty spinnerbait. The paddle tail version is my favorite.

Northland Live Forage Swimbaits

This is another great soft bodied weighted swimbait. It is like the wild eye swimbaits. The Storm baits are shad shaped. The Northland swimbaits look like real forage fish. They look like the fish that swim in the waters in Minnesota and other northern states.

Mann's Lizard

This is a great soft plastic. I like to fish it Texas rigged weightless and crawl it over and through the tops of the weeds. The legs add enough extra movement that gets the bass attention. I like to use grape or June bug in clear water, and Watermelon red or black, blue in darker water.

PIKE LURES

"You can make a pike eat a Banjo minnow when they will not eat any other artificial lure I know of – or even hunks of sucker meat," Babe Winkelman.

Babe Winkelman said the Banjo Minnow was his secret pike bait when nothing else would work. I have tried them a few times, no fish. However, do not overlook the possibilities. Babe Winkelman is a top fisherman from Minnesota who has caught a ton of Pike.

Daredevil Spoons

This lure may be the best lure there is for pike fishing. There are lots of knock offs that try to capture the same action, but they do not have it. The red and white stripe and the five-diamond yellow with black diamonds are the best. You will be glad when you catch a bunch of walleyes and bass on this lure also. This back in the day was one of the best walleye lures. Most will not admit it, but it is still a great walleye lure.

Johnson Silver Minnow

This is one of my all-time favorites. This lure is one of the best lures for pike you will find. It is very versatile. You can fish it in the weeds and on weed lines, and even in open water on structure and flats. The lure will work well by itself but works better if you tip it with a twister tail grub. I use white or yellow. I fish this lure in thick weed, even lily pads and it works fantastic.

I recently picked up one that is painted like the red and white daredevil. I put it on one day and caught a pike on the first cast and a nice bass on the second. Incredibly good bait.

I have also caught many largemouth bass on this lure. I have read it catches catfish as well.

Mepps Syclops

This lure has a similar action as the silver minnow, but more flash and wobble. It is also more erratic in action. However, it is not weedless. That is where the Silver Minnow stands out.

Spinnerbaits

This is the most-used lure for catching pike. Spinnerbaits catch more pike than other lures. They also catch a lot of other fish. Bass, walleyes, and most other fish will go for a spinnerbait. You can catch pike on about any spinnerbait when the fish are active. My favorite ones for pike are black, yellow, and white. Bigger is normally better. Pike are not afraid to go after big baits.

Booyah pikee spinner bait

This is one of my favorite spinnerbaits for pike. This bait catches a lot of fish and it is one of the few that has the twisted wire. I prefer the twisted wire baits. Your line will not move on the wire. It does not move along the wire and get tangled on the cast. Forcing you to waste the cast.

I know they say it is stronger not to twist the wire. They also say it is cheaper for the manufactures to make them without the twist. I like the twist and not having to put something around the wire to keep the line in place. It also comes in great colors and the thinner head makes it rip through weeds easier and with less hang-ups.

This lure is also a great bass spinnerbait, and the double willow leaf blades add the right amount of flash.

Johnson Beetle Spin

This is one of my all-time favorite lures for all fish. If I had to pick one lure and one lure only for fishing, I would pick the beetle spin. It is versatile, it is a spinnerbait and a jig. For Pike I like yellow or black or white. I use it with the split tail or with curly tail bodies. It comes through weeds well and will get bit and hooked better than safety pin type spinner baits. You can also take off the spinner blade and use it as a jig. There is a saltwater version I use for bass and pike. If you want bigger baits, get the salt version. This is by far one of the best baits for all fish, and it catches a lot of pike.

Northland Reed Runner

This is my most-used spinnerbait of this type. It works great for bass and pike and you can fish it anywhere. I like the ¼ oz or ⅜ oz. white shad and I put a 3 in or 4 in Twister tail grub on it. The Canary color with a yellow twister tail grub is great for pike. Made in Bemidji Minnesota.

Mimic Minnow Spin

This is another great spinner that is the same style as the beetle spin. This one has more of a real minnow look, and it comes in more sizes. This bait is also usable in many situations. You can fish it without the spinner, and it is a great swimbait. It will also catch a variety of fish.

CRANKBAITS

Catching pike on crankbaits is easy. If they are active and, in the area, they will bite on about anything. Some baits work better, and some work almost all the time. These are the ones I have found work almost all the time for catching pike.

Rapala original floating minnow

This lure works for almost any fish. Most people say this lure revolutionized. Lauri Rapala saw something that live minnows did that was attracting fish in the 1930s. He tried to mimic it. The original floating Rapala was what came out of his carving and tweaking. This started the company that changed fishing with artificial baits forever.

The original floating Rapala comes in many sizes from 1 ½ inches up to 7 inches. It also comes in a multitude of color combinations to match the baitfish you are trying to mimic. This lure is skinny and has a tight wobble when retrieved. You can fish these lures from the surface down to around 10 feet without adding weight.

This versatile lure is also great for twitching and dancing above weed beds. It is worth using in and around floating timber. If there is one complaint people have about this lure is that it is too lite. It is hard to cast long distance. Because they are built from light wood, balsa, they do not have a lot of weight.

You can add a split shot on the line to get it deeper and make it easier to cast. This is also a great trolling lure. You can troll it on a line, or you can troll it on a downrigger at any depth you want. Pike are hard on these lures. They are light wood. Pike have big teeth and hit hard.

Jointed Rapala

This minnow lure is like the original floating minnow in looks, but the action is different. This lure swims back and forth, more like a short snake. The original thin minnow rapala has a tight wobble from the centerline of the bait. This lure is best fished slow where the slim minnow can work as fast as you can crank it.

Bomber Long A

This is another great crankbait for pike and bass. It comes in a strait and a jointed version. Both works well. The unjointed lure has a tighter wobble. The jointed one has a wider wobble. This lure is similar in action to the Rapala original floating minnow, but it is plastic. Pike love both lures. This is another good option if you are looking for a different action or color combination.

MUSKIE LURES

Bass Pro Shops Muskie Spinner Bait

This is a big heavy spinnerbait, like most musky lures. This bait has dual spinner blades and a bucktail. You should fish it fast. You need to have heavy duty gear and a strong arm to fish this bait. Musky love big bucktail spinners and they love this one.

Blue Fox Vibrax Super Bou Spinnerbait

This is another big dual spinner blade bait. This one has a marabou skirt instead of a bucktail. The marabou holds the shape well even when wet. The skirt keeps the bait higher in the water and it looks bigger.

Mepps Giant Killer

This spinner is my favorite musky and big pike spinnerbait. The bait always runs true and mepps spinners do not hang up like some lower-quality brands. It comes in great colors and the bucktail skirts are top of the line.

Musky Mania Super Jointed Believer
This is a great musky lure that is a crankbait and a soft plastic bait. It has the wavy curly tail with the hard front end with a molded into the body lip. Because of the joint, it has a nice wide wobble that works well fished fast or slow.

Suick Muskie Thriller
This lure has the erratic jerk bait action that muskies love. It also has good side to side action that drives musky and big pike crazy.

Dawg Soft bait lure
This is a great soft plastic lure you can use in a variety of ways. It sinks slowly and can be fished slow or fast. The big waving soft plastic tail draws a lot of attention to attract big fish.

Blade Runner Tora Spin and 1.5 oz spinner
These are both good baits for Musky and big pike. They will also catch large bass. They are both effective. I wish they made the Tora

spin in a ⅜ oz. It would be a killer bait for big bass.

PANFISH LURES

"My favorite bluegill lure, day-in and day-out, is a 1/32-ounce jig with a black, straight-bodied grub," Bill Dance

Live bait

The number-one bait for crappies is live minnows. The best for sunfish is night crawlers, Leeches, minnows and a few types of grubs and insects.

Lindy Fuzzy Grub

The fuzzy grub jig is one of the best jigs to catch many fish. It is a great walleye lure, a good bass lure, and a fantastic panfish lure in the smaller sizes. You can fish it tipped with live bait or plain. One of the best crappie fishing days I have ever had was fishing a fuzzy grub with marabou tail plain, no live bait. A friend and I caught more fish than I counted, it must be over 100. We found a nice school of fish and both got our limit of large fish. It was hard to leave.

Curly tail grubs

These tails on a small jig head are great for panfish. The brighter colors work well for crappies. The darker ones work better for sunfish and bluegills. Use an ultralight rod and light line, cast out and reel it in slowly. Bluegills will follow and attack these baits. Small beetle spin spinners are great for panfish also.

Strike King mini king

The strike king mini king is another of my favorite panfish spinnerbaits. If you need a smaller bait for panfish, this is the one. You can put a curly tail grub on it. This will add enough attractant to make it an amazingly effective bait. It will then attract larger crappies and big bluegills, bass, and pike as well.

Roadrunner jigs

The roadrunner jigs come in a variety of styles and colors. It comes with a marabou, curly tail, a split rubber skirt type tail, or a bucktail in a larger striper version. You can also get it with a Colorado or a willow leaf spinner blade. It has versatility for several types of fish and lots of colors for many fishing situations.

WALLEYE LURES

Ted Takasaki, pro walleye fisherman says the best overall lure for catching walleyes is the Lindy fuzz e grub techni glo.

Many lures will catch Walleyes, some much better than others. Many of the top Walleye lures are also good for other game fish. Some of them are newer. Some have been around for many years and have built a reputation as great fish catching lures.

The lures in this list have proven to be lures that will catch Walleyes. They will catch them under a variety of conditions and seasons.

COTTON CORDELL WALLY DIVER

This is one of those lures that is a great all-around crankbait. The Wally diver is a good casting and trolling lure that will catch a boat load of Walleyes. There is the original version and a newer jointed version.

The jointed version is great with a slow retrieve under the surface. It is also good for bass and stripers fished slow or fast. The lure is also good for smallmouth, crappies, and trout. The best color combinations are chartreuse and perch. Perch are a primary food for Walleyes and Pike.

They also work great when trolling at a faster speed. If the fish are not hitting, try to speed up, go up to the 5-mph range. One thing I hear many people say is that they always run true right out of the package. I have also never had one that did not.

The Wally diver is effective in rivers and lakes. It is also great in wilderness lakes like the BWCA wilderness canoe area, and even in the Great lakes.

Here is a video of a guy catching some nice walleyes on a variety of colors.

LAZY IKE

This is another great all-around lure that was firsthand made in the 1930s. Newell Daniels from Fort Dodge Iowa hand carved all the lazy Ike lures for a couple of years. He got help hand carving them for 5 more years, after that they were machine produced.

The Ike has a very distinct wobble that attracts fish. I have caught Walleyes, largemouth and smallmouth Bass, Pike, crappies and even a carp on this lure. I have one of the old ones that have two sets of double treble hooks on it. It is kind of strange looking, but it has been effective. I have caught many fish on it. I have not used if for many years, I do not want to lose it or damage it. I got it in around 1970. It is still in good shape, and quite different with the double sets of hooks.

There is another remarkably similar lure called the flatfish. It functions much the same and looks remarkably similar. They both catch fish. The lazy ike has a tighter faster wobble**. The flatfish is slower** and has a wider wobble.

Both lures are slow retrieved or slow trolling lures. If you go too fast, they flip over on the side or upside down and do not work. They are great for a slow wide wobble that will attract a lot of fish. This is another lure that will catch a variety of fish. This is a great walleye lure, and one of the best smallmouth bass lures ever.

I have used this lure bank fishing on rivers. Cast out and let the lure drift downstream. let the line tighten and you can let it drift while wobbling into a spot where fish will wait to ambush food.

There is another similar lure called the ok-doke. It has a rudder above the eye hook that gives it a little different action. I have not tried this lure but from what I read it works similar but can be cranked faster and be trolled at a higher rate of speed.

ORIGINAL FLOATING RAPALA

This lure is one of the all-time great lures for many types of fish, including Walleyes. I have used several of them and my favorite is the black and gold. I have used this lure for over 40 years with good results.

When I was a kid, I would go to my grandma's house, she lived on a river. There was a deep pool on the river down from their house. I would go fishing there with my black and gold Rapala and catch pike, lots of them. I learned a lot about fishing there. I learned that you cannot out crank a pike. I would cast and reel the lure as fast as I could, and I would catch tons of pike.

I have also caught several walleyes on this lure. It is amazingly effective at many times, although there is no shortage of Rapala's that catch walleyes. Another great feature of Rapala lures is, they are all hand tuned and tested so they always run true out of the box. Catching toothy fish will mean you will have to tune them occasionally.

I also caught my biggest largemouth bass on a black and gold slim minnow rapala floater. I was fishing in flooded timber on a dead calm late spring morning; I threw the lure out next to a timber and gave it a twitch. I saw a wake moving toward the lure from several feet away. The big female came up out of the water and swallowed the minnow. She was right over 6 pounds, a respectable bass, anywhere, but great in Minnesota.

A good friend of mine caught a 9-pound pike on a silver and black original floating minnow last week. The fish tore the rear treble hook out of the lure. It was hanging by the inside wire.

Here is a nice little video that shows tips on fishing the original floater.

RAPALA SHAD RAP

Many fishermen have said this is the best fishing lure ever made. I do not know if I would go that far, but it is one of the best lures for many types of fish. It is the best walleye crankbait there is. It has the moves and a look that makes walleyes want to eat it.

This lure comes in a multitude of colors. It comes in six different sizes from 1 ½" up to 3 ½ inches and will dive from 5 to 15 feet.

The black and silver and the perch are my favorite colors. This lure is a fantastic casting and trolling lure and runs true out of the box. This is a great all around lure for many types of fish. **Here is a video that shows you how to fish it.**

JIGS

Walleye fishing with jigs is one of the most common ways to go for them. Walleyes go for jigs because they look like food that the walleyes want to eat. The ***Lindy Fuzzy Grub jig*** is one of the most popular jigs for walleyes. You can fish this with a piece of live bait, or the jig alone. The jig has a colored rubber body with a fluffy tail which stays full when it is wet.

You can tip the jig with a minnow, a worm or a leach and catch a lot of walleyes in the right season. Jigs work best in the early season.

They work well when walleyes are in small areas near the bottom or close to isolated structure. Jigs are also great when fishing rivers and other areas of moving water.

Use a 1/4 to 3/8 oz jig. It only needs to be heavy enough to keep it on the bottom. The best colors are techni glo, orange, yellow, lime green, red. Also, any two-toned combinations of these colors. In the early spring or when the season starts in states with closed seasons, use the jigs tipped with a minnow. When the water warms and the fish spread out, you can tip the jig with a minnow, crawler, or leech.

Another great jig is the ***Lindy no snag jig***. Use these jigs when you are in and around weeds. They can be use with a rubber twister tail, but most often used with a minnow in colder water and a leech in warm water.

LINDY RIG

This lure set up works great when the walleye does not seem to want anything else. You can make your own or you can buy them already made for you. The setup comprises a colored hook or a colored jig head on the end of a three ft. leader. On the other end of the leader is a snap swivel. Also, a sinker and sometimes a spinner or colored beads to add to the attraction.

This is the best way to fish live bait for Walleyes. You can use minnows, leeches, or nightcrawlers with this rig.

Berkley Flicker Shad

The flicker shad is a great walleye crankbait. Many people think it is the best trolling walleye crankbait ever. It comes in a variety of sizes and a multitude of colors. You will also catch pike and bass on this lure. This is a lure you need to have if you troll at all.

Lindy Shadling

The Lindy shading is another great walleye crankbait. It is like the shad rap and the flicker shad. The biggest difference is the color patterns and the different wobble. This is another good trolling lure that will work at slow or faster speeds.

TROUT LURES

Lindy Fuzzy Grub

The fuzzy grub jig is one of the best jigs to
catch fish. It is a great walleye lure, a good
bass lure, a fantastic trout lure and terrific
for panfish lure in the smaller sizes. You can
fish it tipped with live bait or plain. This jig is
effective for many types of fish, trout as well.

Blue Fox Vibrax

This is a classic spinnerbait like the Mepps
spinner baits. A little different flash and
colors, but as effective as a trout and all-
around lure. These are also great for salmon.

Mepps Comet Mino

The comet mino is a great lure for trout. It will also catch most other freshwater fish. The Comet mino ranked by Bassmaster magazine as one of the 10 best bass baits of all time. This is another lure that every fisherman should have in the tackle box.

Mepps Inline Spinnerbait

This is another lure that does not fit in one group. Variations of the Mepps spinnerbait will catch every type of fish that swims. I have caught Pike, Trout, smallmouth, and largemouth bass. Also, crappies, sunfish, and walleyes on this lure. This would be one of the two choices of lures I would pick if I could only have two lures for all my fishing. The other would be the Beetle spin. The mepps spinners are not good in weeds. They are not weedless at all, but they are great anywhere there are not thick weeds. You should have at least a black fury or Aglia in your tackle box all the time.

Storm Wildeye Live Minnow

This is another great all-around lure. I have read several reviews that say it works great for rainbows. I have used it several times and have caught bass, pike and even a big bluegill on it. I read reviews of people using it in saltwater and brackish and catching fish.

Flatfish

The Yakima flatfish is another all-around great bait. It will catch most anything that swims. It is a standout lure for lake trout as well as salmon and rainbow trout.

SUMMARY

As you can see, many of these lures are highly effective on several of the main types of sportfish. Which ones are the best all-around lures you can use to catch most of the fish in this book?

Rapala original floating minnow

This lure works for almost any fish. Most people say this lure revolutionized fishing. Lauri Rapala saw something that minnows did that was attracting fish in the 1930s. He tried to mimic it. The original floating Rapala was what came out of his carving and tweaking. This started the company that changed fishing with artificial baits forever.

The original floating Rapala comes in many sizes. From 1 ½ inches up to 7 inches. It comes in a multitude of color combinations to match the baitfish you are trying to mimic. This lure is skinny and has a tight wobble when retrieved. You can fish these lures from the surface down to around 10 feet without adding weight.

This versatile lure is also great for twitching and dancing it above weed beds. It is also effective in and around floating timber. If there is one complaint people have about this lure is that it is too lite. It is hard to cast long distances. They are made of Balsa wood that is very lightweight.

You can add a split shot to the line to get it deeper and make it easier to cast. This is also a great trolling lure. You can troll it on a line, or you can troll it on a downrigger at any depth you want.

You can use this lure to catch about anything that swims. I have caught large and smallmouth bass. I have also caught Pike, Walleyes, Perch, Trout and even bluegills and crappies on the smaller ones. I bet you could even get several saltwater fish to eat this lure. You should always have at least a couple of these lures in your tackle box. A 5 ¼ or a 7" gold body with black back should be one you always carry.

Rapala Shad Rap

Many fishermen have said this is the best fishing lure ever made. I do not know if I would go that far, but it is one of the best lures for many types of fish. It is the best walleye crankbait there is. The Shad Rap has the action and look that make walleyes want to eat it.

This lure comes in a multitude of colors. It comes in six different sizes from 1 ½" up to 3

½ inches, and dives from 5 to 15 feet. This is another lure that everyone should carry in at least 1 or two colors.

The black and silver and the perch are my favorite colors. This lure is a great casting and trolling lure and runs true out of the box. This is a top pick for all around lure for many types of fish. **Here is a video that shows you how to fish it.**

Mepps Inline Spinnerbait

This is another lure that does not fit in one group. Variations of the Mepps spinnerbait will catch every type of fish that swims. I have caught Pike, Trout, smallmouth, largemouth bass. I have also caught crappies, sunfish, and walleyes on this lure. This would be one of the two choices of lures I would pick if I could only have two lures for all my fishing. The other would be the Beetle spin. The mepps spinners are not good in weeds. They are not weedless at all, but they are great anywhere there are not weeds. You should have at least a black fury or Aglia in your tackle box all the time.

Mepps Comet Mino

The comet mino is a great lure for trout. It will also catch most other freshwater fish. The Comet mino was rated by Bassmaster magazine as one of the 10 best bass baits of all time. This is another lure that every fisherman should have in the tackle box.

Lindy Fuzzy Grub

The fuzzy grub jig is one of the best jigs to catch fish. It is a great walleye lure, a good bass lure, and a fantastic panfish lure in the smaller sizes. You can fish it tipped with live bait or plain. One of the best crappie fishing days I have ever had was fishing a fuzzy grub with marabou tail plain, no live bait. A friend and I caught more fish than I counted, it must be over 100. We found a nice school of fish, and both got our limit of large fish. It was hard to leave.

Storm Wildeye Minnow

This is another terrific all-around lure. I have read several reviews that say it works great for rainbows. I use it all the time and have caught bass, pike and even a big bluegill on it. I read reviews of people using it in saltwater and brackish and catching fish.

Flatfish

The Yakima flatfish is another all-around great bait. It will catch most anything that swims. It is a standout lure for lake trout as well as salmon and rainbow trout. It is also a great pike and bass lure. Another one for every tackle box.

ABOUT ME

My name is Steve Pease. I live in the
Northern suburbs of the Twin Cities in
Minnesota.

I wrote my first articles about six years ago. I
have written several hundred articles for
Hub pages and for examiner over the years.
For Examiner I wrote a column for the Twin
Cities on Disc golf. I also wrote a column on

Cycling in the Twin Cities, and one on Exercise and fitness for the Twin cities.

I write on subjects I am passionate about. I write about disc golf, exercise, photography, cycling, fishing. I also write about topics that deal with Christian beliefs.

My father is a retired minister, and he has written many books. I have edited many of them and have them available on my site. The books cover many topics of interest to Christians today. I have also written an Old Testament trivia book on my own.

I have been playing disc golf since 1978 and love the sport. The greatest thing about disc golf is at age fifty-eight I am still extremely competitive. I can beat players much younger than me. Disc golf is a sport you can play at almost any age if you can walk.

I have taken several hundred thousand pictures over the last 35 years. I am always trying to improve my photography. My goal is always to take the best shots I can. I want people to say wow when they look at my shots. I went through the photography course at New York Institute of photography. What I learned from the course and my years of experience was worth every dollar.

The key to being a great photographer is to see things that most people do not see, or in a way they did not see it. My favorite types of photography are landscape, portrait, animals, and infrared. I have shot several weddings. I have also spent hundreds of hours exploring different places. I am always looking for great things to take pictures of.

I have been an avid fisherman since I was a kid. I have had 2 bass fishing boats over the years, but I enjoy fishing for my kayak. I have a sit inside old town kayak, and a sit on top feelfree Moken 12 fishing kayak. I have two old town canoes for going to the boundary waters wilderness area. Or paddling around lakes in my area.

The hardest part about fishing from a kayak is trying to decide what not to take with me. As with most bass fishermen I have tons of equipment, and I always feel I need to take it all with me, in case. Kayak fishing has made me downsize to make everything fit in my kayak.

I spend most of my fishing time catching bass and northern pike. But if I am looking for a good meal, you cannot beat crappies and sunfish. I have spent most of my time fishing freshwater, but I have caught saltwater fish. The biggest was a 380-pound bull shark off Key West Florida in 1985.

I have also loved biking and exercising since I was in my early teens. I like to read nonfiction book so I can keep learning new things all the time. Many of the things I learn I want to share with you and help enrich your life. I want to pass on the knowledge I have learned over the years so others can learn from it.

Thanks again

Check out my book site for other good books.
Stevepease.net

OTHER BOOKS YOU MAY BE INTERESTED IN

Bass fishing boxed set
My 5 books to help you catch more bass

Do you want to know how to go on a new lake and catch bass like you fish it all the time? One of the toughest things for weekend Bass fisherman is knowing where to find fish. The problem made worse when you go to fish a lake you have not fished before. Without the experience, you do not know where to fish unless you have a plan.

Kayak fishing, how to get started and set up your boat

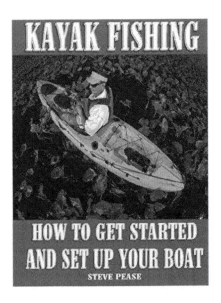

Kayak fishing is growing in popularity by leaps and bounds for many good reasons. Most of the reasons for the popularity are practical reasons that make sense.

Northern Pike Fishing

This book does not to cover every aspect of Pike fishing. I wrote this book so you can take it with you or read it the night before hitting the water. This is so you can have all the best tips and techniques fresh in your mind. It is an easy read, which will help you remember all the best ways to catch Pike when you get in the boat.

I read a saying that makes me think of catching Pike. It said, "God let me catch a fish today so big that when I talk about it later, I don't even have to exaggerate its size. This is a possibility when fishing for Pike almost anywhere they roam. Every cast you throw in Pike waters could get you hooked on the biggest freshwater fish you will ever catch.

Made in the USA
Las Vegas, NV
26 September 2021